# A WORLD OF DIFFERENCE

# DIFFERENCE

S I M O N   J E N K I N S

LION EDUCATIONAL
Oxford  Datavia  Sydnoy

Text copyright © 1988 Simon Jenkins

Published by
**Lion Publishing plc**
Sandy Lane West, Oxford, England
ISBN 0 7459 1337 7
**Albatross Books Pty Ltd**
PO Box 320, Sutherland, NSW 2232, Australia
ISBN 0 86760 930 3

First edition 1988
Reprinted 1990 , 1991

**Acknowledgments**
Our special thanks go to Sue Shaw and the
staff of Tear Fund who have provided most
of the photographs and much of the resource
material for this book.

Other photographs are reproduced by kind
permission of the following: BBC Hulton,
page 16; Camera Press: Richard Harrington,
page 15; Network: Katalin Arkell, page 29;
Rex Features Ltd, page 7; David Simson,
pages 27, 32

Cartoons by Simon Jenkins.

Printed and bound in Slovenia

# Contents

If you would like more information about
Tear Fund's work, write to this address,
enclosing a large stamped addressed
envelope:

Tear Fund
100 Church Road
TEDDINGTON
Middx. TW11 8QE

# A World of Difference

How many times have you heard an item on the news that goes something like this: 'A plane between Tel Aviv and Rome crashed today on landing. Fifty-two people were killed, but no Britons were among the injured'? Or this: 'An explosion in a Spanish disco badly injured three British holidaymakers. Five other people, all foreigners, were killed.'

## SPOT THE HIDDEN MESSAGE

These news items seem to be carrying a hidden message - that people from our own country are more important than people from other countries. The news editor decided that it was more important to mention the three Britons injured than the five foreigners killed.

It seems that the more 'foreign' people appear to be, the less value we place on them.

## LOOKING POVERTY IN THE EYE

We may not want to take the problem of other countries seriously, but it's very hard to avoid them altogether. News pictures of starving children, programmes about droughts or floods, massive adverts in the streets asking us to give money - all these keep reminding us that the things we take for granted would be fabulous luxuries in the Third World.

There have always been people in need, of course. But not everyone has been aware of it. In the time of Jesus Christ, 2,000 years ago, it took even a first-class letter over three months to get from Rome to Jerusalem! Even as little as eighty years ago, it could take

From JAMES STOREY
In Athens

THREE British businessmen were injured yesterday when an earthquake shook Athens. The earthquake, measuring point six on the Richter Scale, struck while most people were still sleeping, at 6.17a.m.

One of the Britons, Mr Richard Dennis, described the quake from the hospital bed where he is recovering from minor cuts and bruises. "The way the ground trembled, it felt as though we were going over the points at Clapham Junction", he quipped. All three Britons are in a comfortable condition.

Many modern buildings in Athens were damaged, and one hotel collapsed, killing at least 20 people. The search for survivors and others continues.

## TEST YOUR horror RATING

Think about this for a moment. Suppose you saw a newspaper report about a gun battle on the streets of a large city. The city might be one of the following:

| CITY | SCORE |
|------|-------|
| Nairobi | |
| New York | |
| Singapore | |
| Sydney | |
| Birmingham | |
| Santiago | |
| Leningrad | |

On a scale between 0 and 10 (where 10 = most interesting) rate your interest-level in the story for each city. When you have done this, ask yourself why you find some cities more interesting than others. Can you see any pattern in the scores you gave each city? Are the lower scores related to the distance of the cities from where you live? Is it because they seem more 'foreign'? Are your lowest-score cities in the Third World (see map)?

The rule seems to be that the closer to home a disaster is, the more horrific we find it. This is one of the reasons why Westerners find it difficult to take seriously the problems of the Third World. It's all so different from the way of life we lead.

months for news of a national disaster in India to reach Britain. Today, it flashes onto our TV screens almost as soon as it happens. TV communication can be so fast that sometimes the first someone hears of their relative being killed in an accident is on the news.

## THE OFF-SWITCH

The trouble with all this fast communication is that it tells us things we may not want to hear. Imagine this. It's early evening, and your family are just getting started on a massive dinner. The TV is on, and suddenly there's a newsflash. A hurricane in the Bay of Bengal has flooded low-lying land, leaving thousands dead and nearly a million homeless and desperately short of food.

What happens next?

■ Your dad gets up and turns the TV off.

■ Everyone is embarrassed, looks at their food and gets on with eating.

■ Someone says something like 'That's terrible', and you start to talk about what you've just heard.

■ Your mum quickly changes the subject and starts talking about the dog, the weather, etc.

■ You wish that they didn't show things like that at mealtimes.

■ Some of your family refuse to eat the food.

■ You all decide to do something about it - however small.

Here are some of the ways people have reacted to this kind of situation...

It's nothing to do with us. They're from a foreign country and they've got to learn to stand on their own two feet.

Sometimes I put money in a box, but it never seems to make any difference. So what's the point?

When I saw those kids – they were shrivelled up – I just _had_ to do something. I felt better then.

We've got problems too. Like unemployment and Aids. Charity begins at home.

That's just the way the world is. They're poor, we're rich.

I felt really guilty after seeing those pictures of children dying in Ethiopia. I gave up eating Mars Bars for a while. But then I thought, 'that's not doing them any good'. But I still feel guilty.

Which of these statements do you feel most strongly in agreement with? Why? Try arguing out your point of view with someone who disagrees.

I'm sorry – I don't seem to have any small change!

## MAKING A DIFFERENCE

Many people believe that the problems of the Third World aren't just someone else's problems, but ours as well. And they've decided to try to do something about it all.

This book is about one such group of people - Tear Fund.

Tear Fund is a Christian organization which was set up in 1968 to link Christians in the First World who wanted to share their resources with people in the Third World. They wanted to do this because they believe that everyone is equally valuable as a human being. Christians believe that men and women are made 'in the image of God' - which means

Hungry people must be fed. But because Tear Fund believes that 'mankind cannot live by bread alone' (for in the words of Jesus, 'life is more than food and the body more than clothing'), it works in partnership with local Christians to help meet people's needs.

that in many ways our characters are like God's character.

This means that *all* human life is important. The death of an unknown beggar in Calcutta is as tragic as the death of a much-loved mother in London. This belief is the opposite of what we saw earlier in the way news is reported. The people at Tear Fund, and in other relief organizations, believe that ordinary people in the Third World are important enough to care for.

Since 1968, Tear Fund has raised more than £60 million to help relieve poverty, suffering and distress. It has also worked to reduce ill-health and malnutrition in more than seventy developing countries around the world. As a Christian operation, Tear Fund believes in helping people in the despair and hopelessness that extreme poverty brings. They do this not only by their relief work, but also by spreading the Christian message.

Tear Fund believes it is important *not* to go into another country and dictate to its people how to run their lives. Instead, Tear Fund works in partnership with the local Christians, and with other organizations such as missionary societies.

## THIRD WORLD?

This map shows the division between the rich nations of the northern hemisphere and the poor nations of the south. The 'south' (excluding South Africa and Australia/New Zealand) is known by various names: the Third World, the Two-thirds world, Developing Countries.

Why do you think each term is used? Which do you think is most suitable, and why? Third World countries used to be known as 'backward countries'. Why do you think this name was dropped?

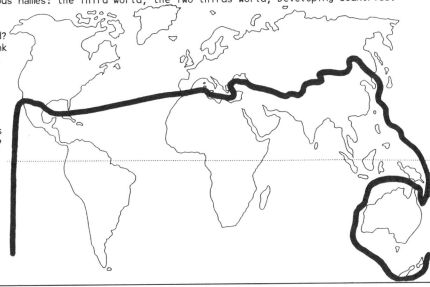

## GIVING YOURSELF

One person who felt that it was his responsibility to do something about the problems of the Third World was the pop singer Bob Geldof. In November 1984, he sat down at home to watch the news, and saw a horrifying report of famine in Ethiopia. Later, he said: 'I felt disgusted, enraged and outraged, but more than all these, I felt deep shame.'

He felt that to do nothing about what he had seen would make him guilty of helping to cause the disaster. Giving a bit of money wasn't enough. 'You had to give something of yourself.' And that is what he did. He gathered over forty pop stars together and recorded the Band Aid hit, 'Do They Know It's Christmas?' And in in July 1985 he organized Live Aid, a rock concert that has been called 'the world's biggest party'. Altogether, these and other ventures, such as Sport Aid and Fashion Aid raised £140 million for famine relief.

# THE · STORY · OF
# TEAR FUND

Jesus said, 'I have come in order that you might have life - life in all its fullness.' People need hope as well as bread to live. Tear Fund believes in helping people to have both.

## How it all started

May 1959-60 was declared World Refugee Year. Many Christians responded to the needs of refugees by sending gifts of money and clothing to a Christian organization called the Evangelical Alliance. A special fund was set up and the money used to help refugees all over the world.

As news of suffering in Zaire or Vietnam hit the headlines over the next few years, more money arrived. The Fund's name changed first from The Evangelical Alliance Refugee Fund to The Evangelical Alliance Relief Fund, then in November 1968 to Tear Fund.

## Aims

From the very start Tear Fund stressed that their reason for existing was to meet both the physical and spiritual needs of those living in poorer conditions.

To achieve this aim, Tear Fund works with Christians from many different backgrounds. Partners include missionary societies, national churches and other Christian organizations. It sends skilled Christians overseas to share their expertise in agriculture, health care, engineering and to teach particular needs.

## Relief and development

Tear Fund has become involved in many different kinds of work:
■ Following a natural disaster or civil upheaval Tear Fund provides money, food, medical services, shelter, water and basic necessities.
■ To improve community life Tear Fund provide money for clean water, medical and health care, agriculture and to create and maintain jobs.
■ Tear Fund links individual needy children, young people and families in developing countries with Christians in the UK who provide regularly for their needs through special sponsorship schemes.
■ Grants are made available to train Christian leaders and provide equipment and materials for overseas churches.
■ Handmade goods from all over the world are imported and sold through a mail order catalogue, by voluntary representatives and through a number of shops. In 1975 Tear Fund formed a company called Tearcraft to develop this enterprise and as a result many thousands of needy people have the dignity and security of earning a living.

## Growth

Tear Fund has grown rapidly. Its support comes from voluntary donations, mainly from churches and individuals who share Tear Fund's beliefs. Today projects are being funded in over 70 countries and about 90 people are working for Tear Fund overseas.

# Another Planet

The people of the Third World might as well live on another planet. Their world and our world are that far apart. We have everyday things that millions of them would find totally alien: hot and cold water taps, soap operas, wall-to-wall carpets, central heating... And they have problems that are completely foreign to us: where to find water, children working all night to earn their family a few pence, no doctor or hospital within two days' walking...

And yet the First and Third Worlds *aren't* on separate planets. We live on the same earth, and we are all part of the same human race. This is why it is important to understand each other. This unit tries to take us from the world we know into the Third World. One way of taking this journey is to think what it would be like to be changed into someone from the Third World.

## FROM PRINCE TO FROG

We've all had to read our fair share of stories where *metamorphosis* takes place. The word *metamorphosis* comes from two ancient Greek words, and it means 'a change of form'. So caterpillars turn into butterflies, tadpoles into frogs, and frogs lucky enough to be kissed, into handsome princes.

The Superman story is a striking example of metamorphosis. The shy, wimpish Clarke Kent, reporter on the Daily Planet, is transformed into 'the man of steel'. He usually makes the transformation by ripping off his Clarke Kent clothes (at super speed) in the nearest convenient phone booth.

9

In the unpleasant stories, it happens in reverse. In a story by H.G. Wells, a young man is robbed of his youth by an old man who tricks him into swapping bodies. And then there are all those horror films where Dracula becomes a vampire, and where respectable businessmen become werewolves.

## FROM FIRST TO THIRD

Probably the most alarming metamorphosis any First Worlder could go through would be to wake up one morning to find that he or she had become a destitute Third Worlder. If this change was irreversible, it would be more shocking than any of the changes of form mentioned above.

One economist, Robert Heilbroner, listed what would have to be ripped out of a typical First World house in order to turn it into a Third World family home. Here are some of the items that would have to go...

beds, chairs, tables, TV, lamps, almost all clothes, all kitchen appliances, nearly all the food, all the taps, bath, loos, all electricity, all...

What about the motorbike?

Then he adds: 'Next we take away the house. The family can move to the toolshed.'

So what is left? This...
- a few blankets, a table, a wooden chair
- one set of your oldest clothes
- a pair of shoes for your dad (but no one else)
- £2.00 in savings for the whole family
- a small bag of flour, sugar and salt

A few mouldy potatoes, already in the rubbish bin, must be hastily rescued, for they will provide much of tonight's meal.

## THE POVERTY CHAIN

There is enough food to feed everyone on Planet Earth. The problem is that our food is unfairly distributed, so that parts of the world have unused mountains of food, while others don't have enough to go round. At the start of 1987, Europe had a whole range of food mountains: there was the 1.5 million tonne butter mountain, and the 16.7 million tonne grain mountain. These mountains were not needed by well-fed Europe, but in other parts of the world, people were dying of hunger.

Why has this imbalance in food and wealth happened?

The causes of world poverty are complex. They are a mixture of geography (poor soil, unreliable rain), politics (international and national corruption), economics (unjust trading by the rich countries), and many other causes. The millions of people caught up in this mess are often completely powerless to escape the chains of poverty they are in.

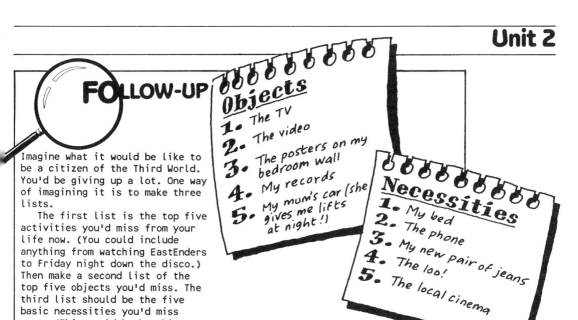

## FOLLOW-UP

Imagine what it would be like to be a citizen of the Third World. You'd be giving up a lot. One way of imagining it is to make three lists.

The first list is the top five activities you'd miss from your life now. (You could include anything from watching EastEnders to Friday night down the disco.) Then make a second list of the top five objects you'd miss. The third list should be the five basic necessities you'd miss most. (This could be brushing your teeth, having a soft bed, anything you consider to be an essential rather than a luxury.)

Here are the three lists made by one school student. They may spark off some ideas of your own...

**Objects**
1. The TV
2. The video
3. The posters on my bedroom wall
4. My records
5. My mum's car (she gives me lifts at night!)

**Necessities**
1. My bed
2. The phone
3. My new pair of jeans
4. The loo!
5. The local cinema

**Activities**
1. Spending at least an hour soaking in a really hot bath.
2. Watching videos.
3. Sinking my teeth into a Big Mac.
4. Holidays abroad.
5. Building up my record collection.

Think carefully before you make your lists. Look back at the items Robert Heilbroner took away from the First World house. Imagine it was <u>your</u> house being emptied.

You could then take this a stage further as a class. Look at your three lists. Choose the object, necessity or activity that you'd find most difficult of all to give up. Then bring in the object (or a picture of it) to show to the class. If it's your cooker, for example, don't drag it along to school! - cut out a picture of a cooker from a magazine.

Then go around the class, asking people why they have made their choices. Does anyone want to change their mind on what they'd miss most. What is a luxury and what is a basic necessity?

**" "** Saudi businessman Adnan Khashoggi's luxury yacht has been put on the market for £19m. It contains eleven suites, a disco, an operating theatre, a helicopter landing pad and a barbecue deck, and the bathrooms are in marble. **" "**

<u>Newspaper Report</u>

This Tear Fund diagram traces some of the causes of poverty. Each link in the chain leads on to the next. It shows how one tragedy leads on to another in trapping people in poverty.

**1** Food shortage and bad diet causes malnutrition.

**2** Coupled with malnutrition, dirty water and poor sanitation cause illness and disease.

**3** Bad health affects children most. Many children die before their fifth birthday.

**4** As children die, parents try to have large families to look after them in old age. This leads to rapid population growth.

**5** Large families leads to poverty in country areas, as more and more people try to live off the same bit of land.

**6** So people uproot and go to live in the towns. This is known as urban migration.

**7** But there isn't much work in the towns. The result is high unemployment. Without unemployment benefit, people rely on odd jobs, recycling rubbish, relatives' help, or even begging...

**8** This means they do not have much money.

**9** As most of a Third World person's income is spent on food, low income means less food. The chain is complete.

**10** A final link is the effect all this has on the thoughts, hopes and feelings of the people trapped in poverty.

The 'Boat People' left Vietnam where they were trapped in poverty. Now they are not allowed to leave their camps, except to return to Vietnam. Tear Fund seeks to help them find a way out.

## MORE THAN SKIN DEEP

Tear Fund, as a Christian agency, recognizes a last link in the poverty chain: 'spiritual' poverty. Think about this for a minute. There are many different sides to you. There's your physical side. There's your sense of humour. There's the way you enjoy your friendships. There's the brilliant way you can score a goal. There's the dark side of you which leads you into trouble.

Christians believe that the deeper sides to our character make up the 'spiritual' dimension in us. It's this that makes you *you*. The spiritual side, according to Christianity, longs for meaning to life, and reaches out to try to make contact with God.

But how does this relate to the Third World? It can be easy to think of the problems of world poverty in terms of numbers, rather than real people. Those who are caught in the poverty chain are people, just as you are. They bleed when they're cut. They have feelings, just as we do.

Tear Fund emphasizes the importance of this in their poverty chain. People do not just starve physically, they also lose hope inside. They become depressed. They feel helpless. They forget how to laugh at a joke. They become too weak to kick a football. They sink into despair.

## EMPTY STOMACHS, EMPTY EYES

This emptiness inside is as much a tragedy as an empty stomach. When Bob Geldof, the organizer of Band Aid and Live Aid, went out to Ethiopia, he saw this spiritual poverty at first hand:

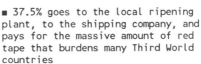

It was not the physical affliction that most upset me, though that was bad enough... what was worse than all that was the look in their eyes. They were glazed, blank and vacuous. They looked but did not see. They were the eyes of people who had given up.

## WHO GETS WHAT?

When you next buy a banana at a local shop, ask yourself who gets the money you've just paid for it. Where does the bulk of the money go? Certainly not to the worker who does a hard day's work in picking bananas, or to the local farmer. The banana below has been split into the percentages people get.

■ 1.5% pays the field pickers
■ 5% goes to the farmer, to cover his other costs and to make him a profit
■ 5% pays for the farmer's fertilizer and transport

■ 37.5% goes to the local ripening plant, to the shipping company, and pays for the massive amount of red tape that burdens many Third World countries
■ 19% is taken by the First World importer (whose label is sometimes on the banana), and pays for further ripening, advertizing and the importer's profit
■ 32% is taken by the wholesalers and by the shop where you bought it

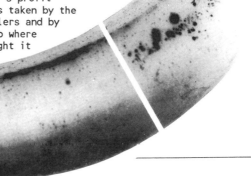

## TEN SHOCKING FACTS

**1** During its lifetime, a child born in the First World will use <u>forty</u> times as much of the world's resources as a Third World child.

**2** By the year 2000, the world population will have grown to 6 billion. 90 per cent of this growth will happen in the Third World, where there isn't enough arable land to support all the people.

**3** In the rich northern hemisphere, approximately 25 per cent of the earth's population consumes 80 per cent of the earth's wealth.

**4** The wealthy nations spend £20 billion a year on helping the poor nations, and £420 billion on weapons.

**5** About 75 per cent of Third World people have no proper toilets or bathrooms.

**6** In Britain, there is on average one doctor for each 650 people. In Nepal, there is one doctor for 30,000.

**7** By its third birthday, a typical Third World child will have had: 16 bouts of diarrhoea, 10 chest and throat infections, an attack of measles and conjunctivitis (eye disease) and possibly malaria and meningitis as well. That's an average of one illness every three weeks.

**8** It is said that rats in India eat enough food each year to feed 100 million people.

**9** In most Third World countries, 80 per cent of the land is owned by a wealthy 3 per cent of the population.

**10** It is said that the people of the United States and Canada, weighed together, are 100,000 tons overweight.

Tear Fund believes it is important not only to feed the hungry, but also to give them hope. Many of the people they encounter have become superstitious about their poverty. 'There is nothing we can do about it,' they say. In breaking the poverty chain, it's vital that people learn that there *are* some things that can be done, so that they can receive help, and start to help themselves.

## RESPONDING TO NEED

Different agencies in the West respond to the needs of the Third World on different levels.
■ **Emergency Aid**. This approach works on supplying food, medical supplies and emergency equipment in a time of crisis.
■ **Development Work**. This approach tries to tackle the problems *before* they build up into a crisis. Development work tries to help poor nations and individuals to develop their resources and skills. The help this gives is longer-term than emergency aid.
■ **Trade Reform and Political Campaigning**. This approach recognizes that if Third World individuals are to survive and build a better quality of life, their countries have to be treated fairly. Many countries are at a disadvantage because the West controls and dominates world trade. The EC countries produce far more sugar than they need, and they sell it cheaply all around the world. This forces the price down and causes problems for those who grow sugar cane in the Third World.

People can try to persuade politicians, banks and companies to change what they do to help those whose voice cannot be heard.

Tear Fund is involved in emergency aid and development work, and encourages its supporters to be involved in working for Trade Reform.

# Clean Water

If someone asked you if you had taps in your home, you'd probably think they needed their head read. It would be like asking 'have you got a brain?' Surely *every* home has taps and a clean water supply!

But here's an incredible fact: only one in seven homes in the world has a piped water supply. And three out of four people worldwide do not have access to clean, safe water. Next to the air we breathe, water is the single most vital ingredient for human life. And yet the majority of the human race survives on a dangerous water supply.

## WATER: THE LIQUID ESSENTIAL

Water is one of those things that we take for granted. We hardly think about it, most of the time. It's only on the very rare hot day, when you don't have enough money for a Coke, and there's not a tap in sight, that you start to realize how much you really *need* water.

At this oasis in northern Niger women draw their water from a well.

# Unit 3

Before the arrival of tapped water in the 19th century, most people in Britain received their water from wells, hand pumps, or directly from rivers. Many people in the Third World still rely on these sources today.

The body of an average adult male contains nearly 38 litres/10 gallons of water. That's about the amount of petrol it takes to fill a family car. If the average male did nothing else but sit still all day, he would lose about half a litre in water by evaporation through his skin. This water loss through the skin would increase six times if he exercised and began to sweat. All this water has to be replaced through drinking.

It might surprise you to know that each person in Britain personally uses an average of 120 litres of water every day. But even that isn't the total figure. An extra 200 litres per person is used by councils, industry and business – in watering parks, keeping fountains going, producing cars, and so on.

In most Asian countries, they are able to use only half that amount. In Africa, only a tenth of the UK amount is available.

Sometimes in Britain there is a mini-drought. There is no rain for weeks and reservoirs run low. The last major time this happened was in the summer of 1976, and it caused widespread disruption. Here are just a few of the effects of what was a quite small drought...

- 1 million people in South Wales had their water cut for seventeen hours per day

- car washing, lawn sprinkling, and paddling pools were all banned

- some industries had to go onto a two-day working week because of cuts in water supply

- people had to draw water from standpipes in the street

- the price of fruit and vegetables rose

- an eight-mile pipeline had to be built quickly to get water into Devon

- football pitches became dangerous to play on

- commuters stranded for ninety minutes in a London tube train smashed the windows and stripped to the waist to keep cool!

- some people secretly hoarded water

- the public were advised to turn their taps off while they brushed their teeth

That was the impact of a short period without rain on a wealthy, highly organized country. Later in this unit we will look at what happens to poor countries that experience severe, long-term drought. And in Unit 4, we will look at one particular drought that helped cause severe famine in Ethiopia.

## 'IT NEVER RAINS BUT IT POURS!'

Northern Europeans complain that they have too much water. One spoof weather forecast goes like this: 'There will be long periods of rain, interspersed with shorter periods of rain.' Complaining about the rain is almost a national sport in places like Britain.

But in Third World countries, rain is usually welcomed. In a drought, no one moans if dark

## A DIG-IT-YOURSELF SPRING

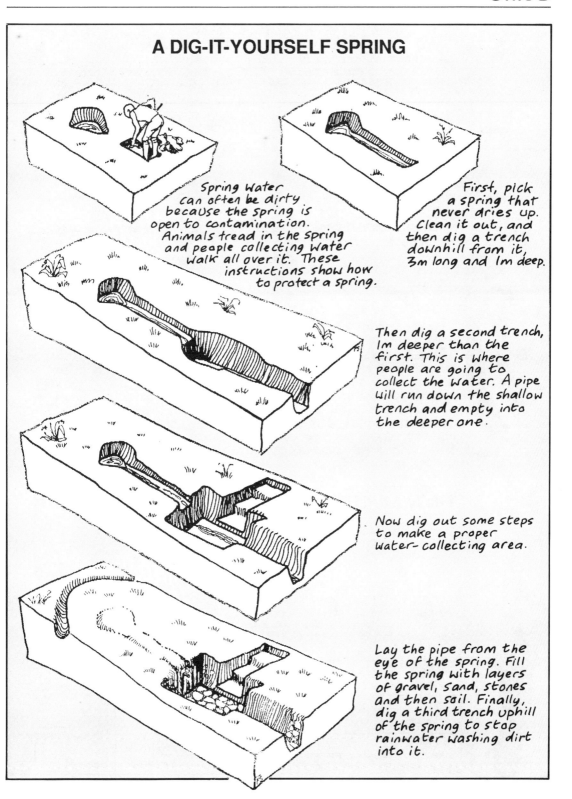

Spring water can often be dirty, because the spring is open to contamination. Animals tread in the spring and people collecting water walk all over it. These instructions show how to protect a spring.

First, pick a spring that never dries up. Clean it out, and then dig a trench downhill from it, 3m long and 1m deep.

Then dig a second trench, 1m deeper than the first. This is where people are going to collect the water. A pipe will run down the shallow trench and empty into the deeper one.

Now dig out some steps to make a proper water-collecting area.

Lay the pipe from the eye of the spring. Fill the spring with layers of gravel, sand, stones and then soil. Finally, dig a third trench uphill of the spring to stop rainwater washing dirt into it.

clouds appear over the horizon. Here is a description of the monsoon rains arriving in India. The speaker is India's first prime minister, Jawaharlal Nehru:

> They came with pomp and circumstance and overwhelmed the city with their lavish gift. The dry land was converted into a temporary sea.

Problems with water arise in the Third World when the expected rains are weak or don't come at all, or when they are too strong. In 1987 there was severe drought in northern India, because of an almost total failure of the monsoon. But in neighbouring Bangladesh, a year's supply of rain fell in just seven days.

They fell just as the Himalayas were releasing millions of tons of water from melting ice.

The result was a torrent of floodwater up to twenty-five feet deep, which immediately drowned 800 people, destroyed crops, contaminated water supplies, swept away villages and affected over 24 million people. This combination of drought in one area and flood next door shows what can go wrong in an unpredictable climate.

## THE THIRSTY EARTH

In some of the more advanced Third World countries, such as India, there has been a programme of digging wells and providing piped water to remote villages. One Indian Christian relief agency has used drilling rigs to sink 600 wells since 1980. But in a drought, everything begins to run dry.

First to go are the taps. Then the shallower wells dry up. This means that you might have to travel many miles to the nearest deep well for your water. In the 1987 Indian drought, water levels

## HOW MUCH DO YOU USE?

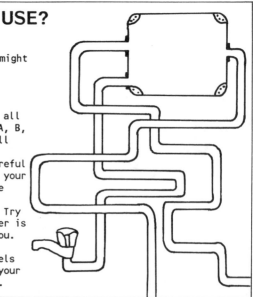

Think about the ways in which you depend on water. These activities might help you...

■ Draw a map of your house showing all the taps you have. Label each tap A, B, C, etc., and underneath describe all the ways each tap is used.
■ Do you waste water or are you careful with it? Imagine if you had to cut your use of water down by half. List the areas where you could cut down.
■ Where does your water come from? Try to find out where and how your water is collected, and how it travels to you.
■ Write 50 words describing to a Martian visitor exactly what it feels like to be terribly thirsty. Make your description as graphic as possible.

## THIRD-RATE WATER

Drought also brings disease. People become desperate to find water, and begin to drink whatever is available - whether it's clean or not. One advert in a newspaper put it like this: 'The water this woman is drinking is spiked with a lethal cocktail of cholera, typhoid and dysentery.'

Three-quarters of the earth's population are in danger from being served this cocktail, as they don't have access to clean water. And here's another shocking fact: 80 per cent of sick people in the Third World suffer from diseases related to bad water supplies. If you think of AIDS or cancer as the big killers, then add diarrhoea. It's the biggest. It kills ten children every minute.

ETHIOPIA 92%  INDONESIA 89%  BOLIVIA 66%  BANGLADESH 44%  BRITAIN 0%

66 We hoped for rain in June, we hoped for it in July, and now we are hoping for it in August. But it's over, it's finished. The drought has reached us. You can see it, you can feel it. 99

INDIAN OFFICIAL, 1987

in some areas dropped down to 150 feet deep. This water could only be reached by the very deepest wells.

Early on in a drought, you might have to travel a mile for your water. But as more and more water sources dry up, you could be faced with a round trip of thirty miles. Some women spend most of every day carrying water in heavy pots on their heads.

## THE NOOSE TIGHTENS

Collecting water is really only the beginning of the problem. What if the water you collect isn't enough to provide for your family and your animals? For millions in Africa during the last few years, the failure of rain has led to this tightening noose of events...
- the harvests fail
- there's no food or water for the animals - they die
- this means people can't provide for themselves
- families leave home and travel miles in search of food
- they end up in large camps where relief organizations try to feed them

- they can't go back home because there is no way for them to get started again

## WHICH IS SAFEST?

Get into groups of four or five. You're in a village in a Third World country. You're all thirsty and are looking for safe water to drink. It's starting to rain. You can see five sources of water:
- a shallow well in the centre of the village
- a fast-flowing river
- rainwater pouring off a roof
- a very deep well with a lid
- a small, dammed-up lake nearby

Discuss where you will get your water from. The answer is at the end of this unit - but don't look until you've decided as a group what to do!

Water is heavy! Try filling the biggest bucket (or saucepan) you've got, and carrying it for 100 m. Women in Third World countries have to carry weights like this over much longer distances...

19

## FOLLOW-UP

In 1987, during the worst drought of the twentieth century, the city of Jaipur in India had its water rationed to one hour per day. But there was one spot in the city where the water poured out. Twentysix water sprinklers were busy ten hours a day, keeping the city's cricket pitch fresh. The England team were due to play a World Cup qualifying match there. While 75 per cent of the crops failed, and the deserts took over what was once farmland, the Mansingh Stadium kept its grass green with water from an underground reservoir. Should they have done it?

Write a letter to the 'Jaipur Sun', protesting or defending the sports decision.

Answer to 'Which is safest?' box

The deep well will probably provide you with the cleanest water - it's far from all surface contamination. But if you don't have a bucket on you to lower, you could try the rainwater. It will still need filtering, though, to make it reasonably safe. Forget the other options - they are all usually <u>very</u> contaminated.

## SAVED FROM THE FLOOD

It was 8 November 1982. In the village of Vankiya in northern India, it had been raining solidly for two days. That evening, the electricity failed and the winds whipped up to 120 mph.

Then at 8 o'clock in the evening, disaster struck. The level of water in a nearby dam was dangerously high. Without giving any warning, the officials at the dam opened the sluice gates. Within seconds, a wall of water eight feet high descended on the village, sweeping houses and people away.

Gobar Madha grabbed his five-year-old son Gabaru and climbed up the nearest tree. But the water surged up around them and the vicious currents tugged at Gobar's son. Gobar had to use both hands to cling onto the tree. He saved his son by the only way he knew, gripping the child's neck and shoulders between his teeth.

For two hours he hung on grimly, his arms and jaw aching. At 10 o'clock the water subsided, and he was able to relax his grip. Gabaru ended up with deep scars from his father's teeth, but they were the scars of his father's love for him. The other fourteen people from their family were drowned.

## FIRST-AID AND SURGERY

What can be done about drought? We might be tempted to think that the problems are too great. Tear Fund and other relief organizations attack the massive problems in several different ways. They try to tackle the immediate problems:
■ They supply emergency food to feed the starving.
■ They bring in medical supplies to deal with disease.
Tear Fund also works on long-term projects. Tackling the emergency problems is a bit like first-aid. But the long-term projects are like surgery - they get to the heart of the problem. They include:
■ Digging new wells to improve water supplies. You might be surprised to know that for as little as £7.64, every Third World person can be guaranteed a water supply for life.
■ Planting trees to make the soil more compact.
■ Providing new, stronger types of seed, and appropriate tools to help people adjust to the great variations in climate.

# Food: Too Little, Too Late

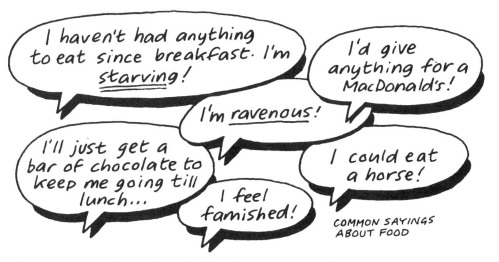

I haven't had anything to eat since breakfast. I'm <u>starving</u>!

I'd give anything for a MacDonald's!

I'm <u>ravenous</u>!

I'll just get a bar of chocolate to keep me going till lunch...

I feel famished!

I could eat a horse!

COMMON SAYINGS ABOUT FOOD

Here are some facts about food that you may not have come across before. Did you know that if you live to a ripe old age, you will have eaten about 20 *tons* of food? Most people can survive without any food for about six weeks.

But with some help, people can survive on very little for much longer. Angus Barbier, a Scotsman, survived for 382 days on a diet of tea, coffee, water, soda water and vitamins. During this time, he lost 134 kg/21 st.

And now here are some *disturbing* facts about food. Up to 10 per cent of European fruit (including apples, oranges, lemons and peaches) is destroyed each year to keep prices in the shops high. The average pet cat eats twice as many calories per day as the average African. Every day, 40,000 people die of starvation. At that rate, the British population would disappear in just under four years.

## FOOD FOR THOUGHT

Something seems to have gone terribly wrong somewhere. While some people feast, others starve. It's one of those facts about the world that no one ever seems able to explain properly. This unit looks at what we think about food, and why it is so unfairly shared out.

Look at the adverts on the next page. Each one of them is trying to sell you food, whether

## WHO'S THE BOSS – STOMACH OR BRAIN?

Most First World people feel that *they* decide what and when to eat, rather than being at the mercy of their stomachs' decisions! But eating habits can be notoriously stubborn. If you think you're a strong-minded person (or even if you don't), try taking on one of these challenges...

■ Go without all your in-between-meals eating, just for one day.

■ Choose a luxury (such as a chocolate bar, or crisps) that

you eat almost every day. Try ignoring it for a week.

■ (This is the big one.) Go without breakfast one morning, and try to eat *nothing* before lunch.

Remember that your experience is only scratching the surface of what Third World people go through.

it's tomato soup, chicken korma or naughty-but-nice cream.

These adverts for food show us how we think of the things we eat. Take some time to look at each of them - some are very cleverly designed and written. Now do some salesman-spotting. Each advert appeals to certain attitudes about food. Can you spot any of these attitudes?

■ Naughty but nice (it's unhealthy, but I'll indulge just this once!)
■ Value for money (we pack in more food than you'd expect)
■ Good eating (this food will make you super-healthy)
■ Cordon Bleu (it may come in a packet, but it's as good as any restaurant)
■ The finest selection (we offer you food chosen for its quality)
■ Lose that flab! (food that slims you down as you eat it - an impossible claim!)
■ Full of flavour (food you buy because of its amazing taste)

What do these ads tell you about *your* attitudes towards food? Do you eat just to keep

your body running, or do you enjoy every sensation in eating a chocolate eclair? Which advert tempted you most? Did any of them actually make your mouth water?

## THROUGH THIRD WORLD EYES

Here is a chart that shows the differences in diet between the First and Third Worlds.

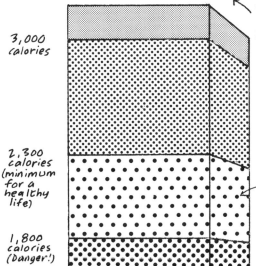

3,000 calories

2,300 calories (minimum for a healthy life)

1,800 calories (Danger!)

The average Briton eats 3,345 calories per day (off the top of this chart)

People in Third World countries such as Tanzania, India and Guatemala, average less than 2,000 calories per day

The United Nations estimates that human beings need an *absolute minimum* of 1,800 calories a day in food to survive. If your food intake drops near or below that figure, malnutrition sets in. The minimum number of calories needed for a *healthy* life is 2,300 per day. Where are *you* on this chart?

Every night, 450 million people go to bed hungry. Each day, 40,000 die from malnutrition. Huge numbers - perhaps one in four children of the Third World - are suffering from malnutrition by not having enough food, or by having the wrong kind of food.

## WHAT DOES HUNGER DO?

When people do not have enough food, or eat the wrong kind of food, malnutrition begins to set in. Those most at risk are children. In many cases, the effects of malnutrition start *before birth*, while the child is still in the womb and is dependent on its mother's diet.

If the process of malnutrition goes far enough, its effects cannot be reversed. One of the most tragic results of too little food is brain damage in young children. Because 80 per cent of

brain development takes place between conception and the age of two, a bad diet in this critical period does irreversible harm.

So what does hunger produce? Blindness, paralysis, deformity, brain damage, disease and death. And it does it by the million.

## FEEDING THE HUNGRY

What do organizations such as Tear Fund do to help feed the hungry? The work they carry out is both short-term (solving the immediate problem) and long-term (planning for the future). See the section in Unit 3 entitled 'First-aid and surgery' for more details. Here are two stories from Tear Fund's files to show the work that is being done among the hungry. They are not dramatic stories but everyday. They show the mundane problems that poor people face all the time.

Aneja is an Ethiopian who earns a meagre living by selling firewood and charcoal. During the drought, his eight-year-old son Ayeley lost weight dramatically and became too weak to walk. The nearest feeding centre was a two-hour walk. Aneja carried his son all the way. Nicki Sullivan, a Tear Fund nurse, was horrified to find that Ayeley was 30 per cent below the weight he should have been for his age. He was immediately put on an intensive feeding programme. This meant three meals a day of faffa, high protein biscuits and extra-nutritious milk, plus vitamins and iron drops.

Soledad de Maria Rivas is a woman with three children, living in El Salvador, Central America. She has been helped by a group called Para Vida, who work as partners with Tear Fund, and run a local health clinic. 'I have learnt a lot about health and nutrition from the clinic and I have also noticed that my children do not have diarrhoea so often now.' Para Vida have also helped Soledad in growing better vegetables for a healthier diet in her garden.

This Bangladeshi woman sells home-cooked food by the roadside to earn money for her family.

## ANATOMY OF A FAMINE

If there is enough food in the world to feed everyone, then why do people still go hungry? Some of the answers to this difficult question can be seen by looking at one disaster - the Ethiopian famine of the mid-1980s. This wasn't just *another* famine. It has been called 'the greatest disaster ever known'. Here are some of the reasons that caused it.

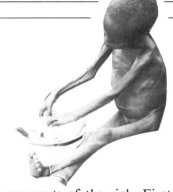

**1** **Bad government**. The roots of the famine go back hundreds of years. For centuries, the Ethiopian people were poor peasants. They worked on land that belonged to a few powerful landowners. They were heavily taxed, and their harvests were often stolen by troops belonging to the landowners. Because the land wasn't theirs, they had no incentive to try to improve their farmlands.

**2** **Bad farming**. Bad government led to bad farming. Ethiopia could still be a rich farming area, if the land was treated differently. Because the people needed firewood, trees were chopped down. Trees do a valuable job by stopping the rich soil being washed away by rain.

**3** **Drought**. We saw in Unit 3 what a small drought can do to a resourceful country like Britain. Ethiopia is not powerful or wealthy. The drought hit it when it was already weak. Several years of drought meant the crops failed, the animals died and people left their homes in search of food.

**4** **International neglect**. In the early 1980s, the governments of the rich, First World countries knew that Ethiopia was plunging towards disaster. But they did nothing, until it was too late. Then in November 1984, the world was shocked by TV pictures of the famine. People felt that something *had* to be done. But the aid was already too late for millions of people.

**5** **War**. To make things worse, at the time of the famine, there were *two* civil wars taking place inside Ethiopia. This meant that planes trying to take food to the starving were sometimes forbidden to fly because of the fighting. While the bullets flew, more people starved to death.

**6** **Exhausted resources**. Even when food did get through, it was difficult to use. Imagine it. You have just been given a bowl of grain to make your first substantial meal for weeks. But you need wood to make a fire to cook it, and water to cook it in. The trees have gone. And there is no water. People tried to eat the rough grain without cooking it, but it tore at their weak stomachs.

All of these different factors (some of which had been around for centuries) added up to the devastation of over 11 million human lives.

> **"** There is enough for every man's need, but not for every man's greed. **"**
> GANDHI

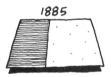
1885

1985

100 years ago, 40 per cent of Ethiopia was covered by trees. Now only 3 per cent has trees. This makes the country vulnerable to drought.

The average young person in Britain can look forward to celebrating her/his 70th birthday one day. But a young Bangladeshi will probably live only to 45.

1st World    3rd World

## FOLLOW-UP

Look back at the adverts. Try discussing these questions...

■ Would any of the adverts be offensive to a Third World person?
■ Having looked at the calorie-intake chart, do you find the thought of 'luxury' food (such as chocolate eclairs) distasteful? If so, why? If not, why not?
■ Suppose that a Third World person could buy any <u>three</u> of the products from the adverts. Which ones would you advise him or her to buy, and why?

## DIARY OF A STOMACH

My Diary 1988 Vol 1

Choose one day in the coming week when you'll keep an accurate list of everything you eat and drink. Here's one way to do it...

1. Use a small notebook and pencil. Keep them with you all day.
2. Start listing things from the moment you start eating after waking up, to the moment you stop eating before going to bed.
3. Write down <u>everything</u>. This is important. Even if you secretly munch half a biscuit in the kitchen when nobody's looking, or suck a polo on the way to school, write it down.
4. Make your notes on what you eat <u>as</u> you eat. Otherwise you'll forget.

The idea is to have a 100 per cent accurate record of everything that goes into your stomach.

When you've completed your diary, there are a number of ways you can analyze it. You may be surprised (or even shocked!) by what you find out about yourself. Here are a few ways of looking at the information you've collected...

■ On another piece of paper, separate the main meals from the in-between snacks, odd biscuits, sweets, etc. How many meals did you have? How many snacks? Why do you eat snacks and how important are they to you? Do you think you could give them up?

■ Look through your diary. What kind of eater are you? Do you eat to live, or live to eat? In the 'Food for Thought' section earlier, we looked at seven different attitudes towards food. Look at these again. Which ones describe your approach to food? Are you a healthy eater, a naughty eater, a bulk eater - or are you a mixture?

# Work: If You Can Get It

How long is the average dole queue? Obviously it depends on how many people in your area are out of work. There are approximately 350 *million* people unemployed worldwide. This adds up to a dole queue that would circle the world over five times. To take just one example, 10 million young people enter the job market each year. And many of them will never find a job.

> Okay. So the Third World's got problems we haven't got, like starvation, bad water and poor medical facilities. But we've got unemployment too! So what's new?

This unit examines what *is* different about work and education in the world's poor countries. But first, what is it like to be unemployed in a First World country today?

## 'KICKED IN THE STOMACH'

That's how one British man described what he felt like after he'd been told his job was finished. 'You feel as though someone's kicked you in the stomach,' Jim said. He had been in his job for many years, and the news came as a complete shock to him.

For Suzie, the experience was a bit different. She had spent most of her time in school dreading not being able to find work when she left. So when it finally happened, she didn't feel shock, just despair. When she couldn't find work after a government training scheme, she thought, 'Is this what life's all about? What's the point?'

Although their experiences were different, both Jim and Suzie had to come to terms with similar problems: not much cash to enjoy; days that seem to go on for ever; the pain of seeing your friends go to work each day. And that was just the start of the list.

## THIRD WORLD UNEMPLOYMENT

Unemployment is a growing problem not just in Britain, but throughout the world. For Third World people, the problems of unemployment are magnified because even those *with* jobs are living on or below the poverty line.

Nishi was the youngest child of a large family and was brought up in a small Indian village. His father was a farmer, and as Nishi's brothers grew up, his father divided his small plot of land between them.

But when Nishi reached working age, there was not enough land left to support him as well.

There was also no other work for him in the village. So at eighteen, Nishi went to Calcutta to look for work.

But Nishi found nothing. And as an unemployed person in a Third World country, he was on his own. There was no social security office for him to claim benefit. There were no job centres to help him in the search for work. To Nishi, facing starvation and total poverty, an unemployed person from any Western country would have seemed incredibly rich.

Nishi ended up begging on the streets, until finally he was picked up by a local gang who taught him a useful skill. Picking tourists' pockets.

## WHAT UNEMPLOYMENT DOES

Unemployment has a massive effect on people and communities. Here are a few of the ways in which people in Britain are affected today...

■ Some turn to crime, partly for excitement and partly for the money.

■ Many sleep longer – up to fourteen hours a day – to escape the pain they feel inside.

■ Many people lose their edge mentally. They find it hard to remember things, or to concentrate and make decisions. One survey found that one in five unemployed people lost the ability to crack a joke.

■ Others keep applying for work and become bitter as they receive rejection after rejection. In September 1987 one man showed Margaret Thatcher 1,000 job applications he had made – all without success.

■ Some give up totally and commit suicide.

■ To boost their benefit money, some unemployed people scavenge rubbish heaps, looking for scrap to sell.

■ There are family tensions. For example, Dad feels humiliated that he isn't 'useful' in the family any more, and lashes out at the other members.

■ Others lose their physical health. They get headaches, ulcers, back problems, and so on.

# SCRATCHING A LIVING

Nishi's experience is lived out by thousands of people every day. Around the world, about 75,000 people per day move to cities in the search for work. But there are not enough 'official' jobs around to absorb such large numbers of unskilled newcomers. The result is the explosive growth of what is called 'the informal sector'.

What kind of job would you be doing if you were working in the informal sector? Here is a small sample of these jobs...

- street barber
- prostitute
- snake charmer
- musician
- street artist

- tailor
- masseur
- errand-runner
- beggar

Sweatshops exist not only in Third World countries, but in many parts of the Western world too. Workers are paid meagre wages for long hours of exhausting work. This clothing factory is in East London.

If you were desperate for money in a Third World city, you could also choose a career in crime by joining the underworld. It's estimated that 40 per cent of working people in Calcutta are doing these jobs (and others) in the informal sector.

If everything failed, you would probably finish up in one of the shanty towns, scavenging for food among the rubbish. You would have reached the last-but-one stop on the poverty line. Next stop, death through starvation or disease.

# 'SWEATED' LABOUR

Even where there is work in the Third World, it can mean long hours for very little money. A rich landowner or a rich factory owner is easily able to take advantage of the poor. He knows that they are too weak, and need his money too badly, to argue with him about wages. Factories where workers are treated in this way are called 'sweat shops'.

In Hong Kong, there are many sweat shops, ranging from printing works that offer cheap prices by underpaying their workers, to clothes and toy manufacturers.

In India, young children are used to make beautiful, patterned rugs. Their small fingers can do the intricate work more quickly than an adult, and they don't demand high wages. These children often work over twelve hours a day in dim rooms which affect their eyesight. The rugs are sold for thousands of pounds in the Western world, but the children receive next to nothing for work that an adult would find exhausting.

In South Africa, miners are forced to live in hostels, apart from their families, for ten months every year. The work is brutal, the wages low, and their children grow up without knowing their fathers. But they do it because there is no other way to support their families.

Many Christians are outraged that people are treated in these ways. Lord Shaftesbury in the 19th century campaigned against the cruelty of making children work in mines and in factories. In 1947, the Ten Hours Act was passed which limited the time children could work per day to *ten hours*. William Wilberforce, another Christian reformer, campaigned successfully to abolish the British slave trade.

Tear Fund, along with many other relief agencies, follows in the footsteps of people like Shaftesbury and Wilberforce.

## TRAINING FOR LIFE

Tear Fund works in two ways to combat some of the evils of unemployment. They try to encourage...

- education
- small-scale, cottage-industry jobs.

## A MEXICAN FARMER

Lareano Loesa is a thirty-seven-year-old farmer. He and his wife have five children. He makes his living by growing sisal on his land in Mexico. Sisal is the only crop he can grow, because his land is dry and rocky. (You've seen sisal if you've ever used twine to tie up a parcel.) But the price of sisal has dropped recently. People are using other types of string (nylon, for example) to tie their parcels. This means that Lareano only makes as much money as he did five years ago. What's wrong with that? Prices in Mexico (including the price of food) have risen 500 per cent in the last five years.

## 1 EDUCATION

Think how education might make a difference to a Third World person like Nishi (see 'Third World unemployment'.) If Nishi had learnt how to read, there might have been a number of jobs he could have tried for. If he had learnt some maths, he would have been better equipped to learn how to trade. And for people who end up in sweat shops, a better education would make it harder for their bosses to cheat them. It's been said that educated people are hard to fool and hard to suppress.

One Tear Fund project is running in Naivasha, a village in Kenya. Young people from Naivasha were leaving home with no skills and heading for the cities, where they drifted into crime. The local churches were concerned, and built a polytechnic for the village. Tear Fund provided some staff, and money to help with the building. Now the young people learn skills such as carpentry, farming and animal health, which will help them find good work.

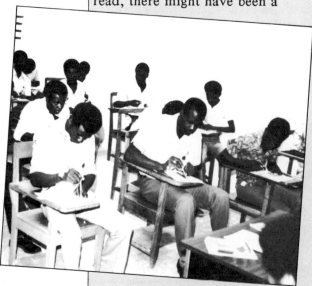

## 2 COTTAGE INDUSTRIES

One branch of Tear Fund is called Tearcraft. Tearcraft makes it possible for people in the Third World to sell small, hand-made goods in the Western world.

Many people in the poor countries of the world make their own pots, baskets, rugs, mats, etc. Often it is the women, who are not allowed to do paid work, who use traditional skills in making these objects for their homes. But why not use these skills as a way of earning money? The name for this type of work is 'cottage industry' - small-scale employment that is based in the home.

This is what Tearcraft does. It encourages people to produce the goods, and then ships them overseas where they can be sold in richer countries. Working at crafts in this way is often the only source of income for widows and single women in areas where they are not allowed to own land or get a job.

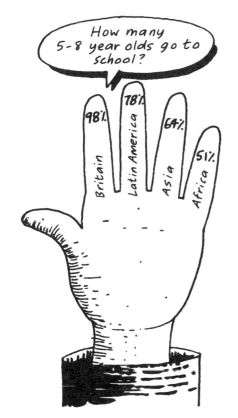

How many 5-8 year olds go to school?

Britain 98%
Latin America 78%
Asia 64%
Africa 51%

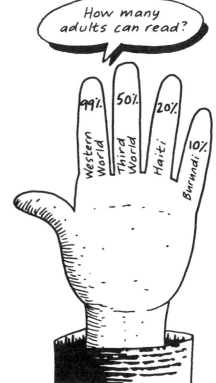

How many adults can read?

Western World 99%
Third World 50%
Haiti 20%
Burundi 10%

# Unit 5

## MAKING A DIFFERENCE

Looking at the way people in the Third World live - and die - isn't just another subject to learn about. Most people find starvation and poverty uncomfortable reading, or embarrassing viewing. This is probably because we feel inside that their problems are in some way *our* responsibility. Hearing about the Third World challenges us (or even *dares* us) to do something about it all. Here are some of the ways people respond...

The **'I'm too small' midget approach**. It's all too big - mass starvation, drought, the greedy rich countries, unemployment... What difference could *I* make?

The **packed suitcase approach**. I think I'd like to spend at least some of my life working in a way that would help. I'm going to find out more about it.

The **Mars Bar response**. I'm going to give up something I really like for a month and send the money I would have spent to a relief agency. At least it's something...

The **'Dear Parliament' attitude**. A few of us are gonna get together and write a letter to our MP. We want to know what the government is doing about the Third World's problems.

The **crocodile tears reaction**. I think it's terrible, what goes on. It makes me feel really sorry for them. Now, what's on after the News?

The **eyes open method**. This is so important I'm going to write off to an agency to get their regular newsletter. At least I'll know then what's going on.

The **head in the sand method**. really rather forget about the whole problem - it's too heavy to cope with.

It's been said that in life generally we can either be part of the problem, or part of the solution. Our response to the Third World can put us on either side - helping or hurting. Where are you on this scale of responses?